THE LOS ANGELES GARDENING GUIDE

by Thea Rosemary

Published January 11, 2021.

Second paperback edition; first reprint by IngramSpark: September 2021.

ISBN: 978-0-578-82860-2

Cover design, illustration, and layout by
Thea Rosemary.

Copyright © 2020 by Thea Rosemary.
All rights reserved. No part of this book may be reproduced or used in any manner without written permission of the copyright owner except for the use of quotations in a book review.

POISON & PESTICIDES

garden gnomes ... 8
holding on to hate ... 10
homebody ... 12
coupled up ... 13
backyard play ... 15
carnivorous ... 18
cloud crossfire ... 20
to be tangled in enchantment ... 21
temporary tulips ... 24
a trip to the museum ... 25
lust of the sun ... 26
walks along the party ... 28
twenty one birthdays ... 30
in the crisis of identity ... 32
public displays of dissatisfaction ... 34
the ocean between me and me ... 36
one sided driving dialogues ... 38
air bubble request ... 40
pre-isolated beliefs ... 41
dried bouquet ... 44
morning coffee order ... 46
how to be an artist ... 48

SUNSHINE & GROWTH

plastic plants ... 52
mistaken dandelion weeds ... 53
midnight moth ... 58
curling at the edges ... 61
root rot ... 63
under the blue moon ... 65
not so small south bay town ... 67
window shopping ... 71
the writers war ... 74
at the scissors edge ... 78
a screenwriter's daydreams ... 81
post-isolation ideals ... 84
main character syndrome ... 86
a letter from your medication ... 90
coastline horizon ... 92
nice to meet you ... 95
the end is over ... 98

POISON & PESTICIDES

GARDEN GNOMES

estranged travelers wander past a white gate
engraved with angels
and the french fleur de lis.
a woodpecker has carved a hole
in the top right corner
where the wood has gone soft with rot.
passers-by press their eyes and lips to the spot,
searching and murmuring
to understand what lies inside.

no one could ever imagine the vastness of growth.
willow trees swaying like ballerinas,
catching wisps of the sunlight
to splatter onto the moss-ridden ground.
swallowtails and viceroys gather
in the bougainvillea,
while chirps gather in the newest crow's nest.
feathers fall from the ficus,
littering the forgotten brick path
spotted with cigarette ashes and lowe's receipts.
garden gnomes sit happily on the bench side,
the legs carved to be kicking
in the midst of delight.

this garden—

it's a fairy tale from a storybook.
so ample with life
while the house remains alone;
rotten and hollow like the fence
that tries to keep everything inside.

HOLDING ON TO HATE

the grass shimmers in the morning light,
crystalline like the innards of a geode.
passing yawns think of it as nothing more
than the morning dew.
but me?

you see,
i knew it was poison crusting over the blades
like the blood between carrie's legs.
i told my family to close the windows
so they wouldn't breathe in the rot
that smelled of spoiled soil and human decay.

i held a mask over my face
as i sprayed the garden in the waning light of day—
a child completing their monthly chores
in the eyes of any peering neighbors.
heat burned my neck,
seared the ridges of my spine
as the hollywood sign glimmered
on the backbone of suburbia.
i moved slowly,
until the sun couldn't keep awake
and every shard of daylight
splintered and fell away.

i was left in the quiet arms of the dark,
where crickets chirped and distant crows wept.

when everyone had finally fallen asleep.
off the mask went,
thrown and left in the weeds
like the pillar of a familiar face
no one could quite place.

down on my knees,
breathing in deep,
i soak in the poison and
feel everything inside of me light up.
brighter, brighter, brighter,
until the firewood crackles and breaks.
ashes cloud my lungs and it's
oh
so
sweet.

the pesticide is a killer,
and i'm at the guillotine.
i'm glad no one is looking
as i lay my head under the falling blade.

HOMEBODY

we collect gardens like photos—
hanging on the walls to flaunt to guests.
we cherish flowers like people,
placing them in vases
never to grow again.
but these blooms must be left outside
to grow on their own
until they have sprouted every petal
and each little leaf.
yet we feel the need to have something pretty
on our bedside.

we pluck them from their homes
before they are ready;
prematurely in their growth.
that is why,
in those elaborate vases of yours,
the flowers go cold,
reeking of death.

still we say,
you're so pretty.
there is no response;
we hold our breath from the stench.
you're all mine.

COUPLED UP

broken hearts have a way of finding each other:
sharp edges that drip in blood,
we leave pathways to be followed and found.
underneath gray skies that were once pulsing
with pastels and radiant beams of light,
we lay scattered across the forest floor
in jagged pieces,
as though we are remnants
of a homicide.

broken hearts have a song:
a mating call that finds those
who have wandered too far down a distant hall.
turning around and falling down the rabbit hole,
we tumble into a wonderland of tattered ribbons
and broken bouquets,
tying each other into tumbleweeds
only to tell each other
how beautiful our bodies were crafted.
as though our skeletons were carved
to be a puzzle piece,
and we are to spend decades searching
for the missing shape.

broken hearts have a secret:

though we shout loud of our despair,
scrawling unfinished thoughts
among the concrete we walk,
i must admit,
we adore the rush of shattered dreams
and shadowed memories,
for there is nothing more inspiring,
than a broken heart.

BACKYARD PLAY

fill me up to the brim like the balloons you gathered
for your childish wars.
the smell of rubber burns like the drunken tire marks
you left across the 405 freeway.

what once felt like the warmth
of the hearth i never had
has become the broken house
you said we would have.
despite my pleas asking you to slow down,
chew on your words and think before you speak,
you forgot all i said and left me spellbound.
i blame myself for falling prey
to those insecure smiles—
those eyes full of lies.

i blamed you for my fall,
for the mask you put on
before i'd meet you in the mirror
and the lines you stacked on the glass tabletop
behind my back.

but the truth is i loved you,
and in your sad, pathetic way,

i think you loved me, too.

i know you did—
you forced yourself to feel fond,
elderly sort of affections
to try to make your life feel less broken.
i know this because you tell every girl you date
that you can't wait to get married.

it's sad how my family welcomed you in
as one of their own,
and even though you appeared to dance in
without fear,
you were always on your tiptoes—
hiding knives in the pockets of your ripped jeans.

i thought the blades had dulled
being in better company,
but you were sharpening them in the shadows
of your dusty car.
i should've seen them gleam;
that the idea of the broken person
who turned beautiful
was not who you were,
and maybe not someone
you could ever be.

if you ever see this and wonder
why bits of you are found in my prose,
it is to ask—
to plead—
to think twice now,
before you pull another
into the water balloon war zone of your brain,
looking for a woman to call *mom*
so you can finally have someone
sing you a goodnight song.

CARNIVOROUS

a growl from the night
resonates from deep inside
the shredded remains
you left behind.
ribs split like a mosaic,
hair pulled from my scalp like weeds,
the shadows of your jaw, your teeth,
flicker like the village bonfire.

now your smile has stretched into fangs,
and in the gleam of your eyes,
i witness a plea asking me
to bare my teeth.
a beast for a beast, you said,
this is what is meant for you
and me.

so we feast upon one another,
trying to fulfill this divine hunger.
we send howls against the moonlight,
making orion's belt quiver.
our bellies are full,
but the lust for more forms a rumble,
from your balding haunches
to your shoulders filled with fleas,

up to the rotting stench
of your sticky-sweet tongue
always thirsty for more.

to tear each other to pieces is much better
than spending any moment apart.

how frightening it is
to hear the click-clack of your claws
that were never mine,
but yours all along.

CLOUD CROSSFIRE

dangling in the clouds,
like cupid himself,
i have been strung out over lost lovers.
romance torn apart,
chasing kites of color
on wings plucked to bare skin,
the cold bites my eyes
and rips me apart from within.
rainbows twisted like ribbons
on a valentine's day gift,
sweet and silky like the satin drawers from within—
the glimmer of the string threatens to fall,
begs to be held.

as the rainbow caresses my fingertips,
promising to carry me to flight,
the urge to wrap myself around it—
i want more.

to be so infatuated,
you don't even see the arrow
piercing your heart,
breaking your spine.

who needs to walk when you have wings?

TO BE TANGLED IN ENCHANTMENT

out in the woods, i wandered lost.
a swathe of leaves dangles before my eyes.
and here i am, left blind.

then i heard your song.
much like a siren luring a sailor,
i followed your call to a forest
made entirely of silver and gold.
your wings like the lunar eclipse,
all i saw was the light
you so delicately weaved.
hypnotized by the ember in the dark,
you were my guide, i believed.
my new meant to be.

it was the lovely rhythm of your song
that left me in a dreamlike haze.
then the leaves fell away
and the sunlight spilled through—
my eyes burned with such might.
from the scorched greens to the fallen trees,
this is not what i thought it to be.
your song was not the pretty hymn of a lark,
but the drill of a woodpecker
that skewered my vision and blurred

the hairline fractures in my mind
telling me this is all a lie.
screaming for satisfaction of the truth,
the trees burned like coals.
there began the collision of a wildfire.

as the forest finally extinguished
and the ashes fell away,
i found you in a thrush of cold beetle dung.
how tiny you were
with a nose so long,
you would stumble over each step—
just a pesky little woodpecker
trying to cast a nasty spell of a song.

how does it feel to live in this fantasy
where you are the bird
and i am the prey?
to think you are so far above me,
high off the air and the euphoria
of your temporary flight.

check your wings, little one.
you think yourself grand enough to fly for eternity,
balanced on the whispers of the sky
that you fail to see
how your wings have snapped

in twos and twos—
so incredibly broken and skewed,
you are so awfully
inhuman.

TEMPORARY TULIPS

how deadly the thrill of a new bloom.
the vibrant colors of petals too soon to flourish
intoxicate my sight.
the world becomes a kaleidoscope
of rainbows and star shine,
all because of this poison
you have produced;
found in the honey of the flowers—
in the pollen stuck on the honeybee's knees.

i know in the passing days,
the leaves will curl and fade.
but darling, how i love
to savor this little bud of delight.
like the wink of spring
with glittering pink blooms and emerald green vines,
we have grown sickeningly captivated
by these sights.

surely like the brink of summertime sunshine,
this, too,
shall fade away.

A TRIP TO THE MUSEUM

now look here—
look at this delicate birdcage,
made of wilted wood and frayed twine—
it's hanging on the last grapevine.
pluck it sweetly,
hold it between your fingers gently,
as though it's virgin mary's
great white lily.

see the feathers fluttering
from deep inside,
bright like snowfall on the hillside
caught on the cusp of dawn.
the dove within coos
for a song of love.

here's the key.
hold it close;
hold it near.

once the dove falls into your palm,
this love will only last
for so long.

LUST OF THE SUN

wild under the willows,
a satin skirt billows;
teasing the moonlight
with shining glimmers of white.
in the rustle of the wind,
as the curtain of leaves pull apart and sway,
the couple can be seen dancing,
intertwined,
refusing to pull away.

in this promised land,
the young couple must stay hand in hand.
bound by the breeze,
dark hair swirls and swallows
while pale eyes gaze.
smiles so bright,
the sunshine appears to be in a fright,
spewing out dabbled beams of light that scatter,
shattering the fragile leaves.

he told me this would be our summer love—
the light would find us,
guide us to the ocean we had grown
so fondly to know.
how romantic a time

as sweat coats the hairline,
and the salt of the ocean stings and blinds
the eyes.

i hold you above water,
blinking the tears from my sight,
while you allow me to sink under.
yet you smile as though we
are the pair of lovers
under the willows,
madly in love,
like this will last forever.

all i am left with
is a cracked frame and a sun-stained canvas
to be put on display for others to behold,
while i remain at the back of the stage
removing willow leaves
from the crooks of my teeth.

WALKS ALONG THE PARTY

i always thought it would be under a sea of stars
i would find a twinkle of the surreal—
the fantasies from all of my favorite childish
make believe stories.
instead, i find myself stuck in a snow globe
where i am happiest and saddest
furthest away from everyone i know.

peel away the paper sky scrapers
and the cardboard oceanside horizon,
for i find it all to be a mirage
to retain the shimmer
of this quote on quote,
lust for life.

nobody warned me of the contemporary fantasies
that would take flight.
i forgot how to walk among others
and tell them i'm fine.
i try to puppeteer to their drunken sways
and rambunctious laughter that stains
the air until midnight.
these illusions must exist to satisfy
their delusions,
while I remain high on the dream

of waking up in a faraway place,
under a different face and name.

my existence feels accidental.
sometimes I wish nobody was around
to ask me to stay.

TWENTY ONE BIRTHDAYS

swarmed with bouquets tied up like ribbons,
and shimmering papers and plastics
with a side of sugary, sweet
pink frosted cake,
the light of neon-colored candles
burn the hairs from my face.
confetti caught in crow's feet
as smiles gleam from the corners of my eyes—
make like a magician,
allow me to make my happiness
reappear.

painted red lips press pastel cheeks
into a grin too wide to hide.
sing softly while i sit at the table side,
sipping on youth as it slips away.
innocence falls like the roses
trapped in a glass vase—
a gift from a friend
who will soon become a stranger.
hope fades like the convenience store mascara
found in my mother's old makeup supplies.

here i go,
watch me blow out the candles.

ghosts at my side,
eager for change—
for the hope of a wish
that will never come to be.

IN THE CRISIS OF IDENTITY

a scramble of words simmer at my bedside,
buttered like eggs on toast.
hunched over as the house falls into a lull,
i feel myself freeze solid,
lost in the war zone of stale winds
and clogged construction stench.
i force myself over to my side,
reaching for a fork and a plate—
maybe even a napkin—
anything to keep these sonnets
from getting soggy.

with prose like sugar and similes
like cinnamon,
the flavors lather and blend,
prodding me to take a bite.
good enough to be in a vegan cafe,
but not the fancy kind you would find
in downtown la.

i place the plate on the window
as i wander about my day.
too much time goes by,
but i am nothing of the wise.
the sugar grows hard and cold,

while the spices lose all flavor.
dust collects on the ruffled hem
of the crust,
while the skin remains golden.
not even the birds will stop by to sing;
nor the rats, who will eat
just about anything.

to some,
the meal may as well be glass,
while the decay pulses through like tree roots.
but to the rest of us—
what a perfect treat.

pass the whole platter and watch
as i eat it down to the cracked glass of the plate,
only to gag and retch
until i become sick.
riots will form and burst,
asking for ingredients to shift and change—
a reform of sorts—
you see what i mean?

and here i've been,
just trying to write prose.

PUBLIC DISPLAYS OF DISSATISFACTION

i used to be quite sad,
but instead of going home and writing it down,
i'd go ahead and shout it out
to the whole town.
spit my insecurities into the gullet
of a chipped seagull's beak,
for it to swallow and
throw up over the cars
that have been parked too long
on pacific coast highway.

the morning bird calls
that once chimed like bells,
sit deep in my chest like the warfare
of world war iii
that may never actually come to be.

perhaps if i shout out my pain
into the pixels of my iphone screen,
my words will hit the trending page.
maybe then you will understand
the way you destroyed my faith
in human individuality;
the pain that comes when others

refuse to acknowledge
the meaning of honesty.
without thinking twice,
you won't recognize
the little face inside the bubble
you used to wake up to,
promising marriage
and a best friend for life.

i'm thinking now
you only saw the number of followers and thought
you found someone exquisitely unique—
a prop for your instagram photos;
a lure for the pretty girls
on your social media feed.

i don't know if this will make you happy,
but i've turned this pain you brought to me
into a chapter's worth of poetry.

i don't feel sad anymore;
just used, insecure, and angry.

thank you for leaving me.

THE OCEAN BETWEEN ME AND ME

i've lost my appetite to go home.
i'd much rather drive down vista del mar
with tears in my eyes,
begging the gps for directions
on where the fuck
i'm supposed to go.
sorry for the language—
i've been crying for hours now.
i would like to be in my bed alone.

not really though,
because here i am listening to this sad,
indie band called seafret,
thinking of how i can turn this pain into prose.
maybe then my life will have a purpose,
you know?

you know what i mean,
when you can't remember the silhouette
of what you tell yourself and your friends
is home?

it's not my family's fault—
they keep the house warm
with tenderness and love.

you see, it's me and only me,
for i fear i have gone too cold.
not like ice cream the kids are carrying
on the sand below,
while i sob from the pier in my little blue car—
that is too delicate,
too soft.

i have become an iceberg that refuses
to be moved by the current of my higher self,
melting in the heat of my depression
and my deep-seeded fear of abandonment.
i try to powder my lips in sugar,
lick them until they're chapped
in hopes i will remember what it feels like
to not only be home,
but to stand on my own,
knowing that even if life falls apart,
i am here.

i am my walls,
my hearth,
and my twin size bed.

i am my home,
but i cannot find the road.

ONE SIDED DRIVING DIALOGUES

what's the point of life
if every person you meet
eventually disappoints you?
finding someone who doesn't.
how do you do that?
by not disappointing yourself.

                    isn't it strange how we mourn people
                        that were never truly ours?
                            strange how that loss
                      is the most agonizing of them all.

i know love is nothing more
than a mere chemical reaction,
but i achingly wish for love
to be a product of the cosmos—
an alignment of stars,
the golden halo of the sun—
something magical
that we cannot explain.
but it's not.

                what do you mean when you say you love me?
                    is it true that you love this muddle of tears,
                                so filled with fear?

doesn't seem like it.
or is it the title you love to carry—
the idea that someone is yours
and you are theirs?
i don't think he ever loved you.

at least if someone
doesn't fall in love with me,
i'm bringing them one step closer
to their love story.
what about yours?
what about mine?
don't you want love?
i think loving was meant for others,
not for me.
that's sad.
it's okay,
please don't pity me.
don't think about it too much.

AIR BUBBLE REQUEST

i only follow people i know,
so please don't be offended
when i inevitably say no.

maybe this is why i find it difficult to date—
how quickly it all develops:
the bitterness and the hate.

i've found love to be the pyre of my life,
scorching the sands beneath,
and the skin of the sky above.
it's beautiful until the entire thing peels
like my old pink bedroom paint.

after convincing myself i am devoid
of maintaining human connection,
i will cover the ash-stained walls
with picture frames filled with friends
who will tell me they love me,
but secretly laugh
about my intimate
insecurities.

PRE-ISOLATED BELIEFS

i have this theory
i am not what society wanted me to be.
what used to be, and occasionally
still resurfaces like an allergy:
a fear for not fitting into the womanly mold—
a condo with some kids a few blocks down
from my childhood house in my hometown.
to be please, my dear,
anything but the old,
single,
cat lady.

scorned and burned,
skin turned around to be displayed
from the inside out,
hands clawed and begged for more—
more about me and my proclaimed destiny.
as i tiptoe into the twenties,
my mind whispers
i am doing something wrong.

my charcoal stained fingertips
fail to fondle a lover's hand;
my twisted tongue stays warm between my lips
as i sing along to this sad song

from the faded name
on my middle finger.

i cry in the bathtub so nobody hears me,
as my heart thrums with love
for the inanimate and fantastical,
failing to hum for another who says
we belong together.
the broken pieces remember
what the last one said.
i think they're starting to realize
how temporary this concept of love
seems to be.

it's made me want to leave
this whole world behind sometimes—
the thought that love does not exist
for me, or anyone.
that we're all wandering around aimlessly,
hungry for a harvest that will never come.

for too long
i've tried to hold onto the lines of a script
for a young love that tears me apart—
that lasts for years,
until something tragic
breaks us apart.

perhaps it will happen,
but i'm not waiting any more to find out.
everyone that's claimed to have loved me
finds their burning ember
after i set them free.

when i think about it,
sometimes my tears twinkle brighter
than the select stars that shine
through the city smog.
photos of me are replaced
for the next face;
memories are remade in the places
i told them belonged deeply to me.

i guess it's okay,
they found their happiness
and in some strange way,
it was because of me.
i like to think that i am the bridge
that carries wanderers to the homes
they've dreamed of;
the journeys they thought
to have only existed in fantasies.

they found their love;
it was because of me.

DRIED BOUQUET

let me tell you,
those who loved me,
loved me wrong.

i've come to learn in these years,
romance is a blooming dandelion
asking for a wish that may never come—
i think it's always a little wrong
that nobody can ever love me fully,
or how i want to be loved.

hopeless, though i find beauty
in the budding nostalgia
that comes with faded out color slides;
knowing to collect tears in a jar
to look upon years later,
as i smile in the eyes of the beholder,
holding hands with the broken hearts
that have been instilled
with the first breath of the new world.

i've been trying to write this ending
for some time now,
and i think it goes like this:
i was not created to love or be loved

by anyone else.

MORNING COFFEE ORDER

light on the ice, please.
i need to stay warm to house the home
for my lover who says i've gone cold.
like the sixty two degree nights
they cannot handle in their bare skin,
they tell me my face has gone hard—
rock solid.
it's more than a case
of resting bitch face.

i apologize while trying to rip the blade
out of my knife;
softening my eyes
while i beg for another try.
but like the post-climate change autumn rain,
i cannot seem to remain in cover
where i am forthcoming
of my pain.

watch as the storm drags
into march madness and everyone huddles
like penguins in their puffer jackets,
in which i refuse to wear.

maybe that's why you always say

i have this way
of coming off angrily.

i stand before you
in a thrush of the almighty beauty
of the truth.
yet you frown because my words
were not an encasing of silk,
but rather a gripping of fingers
around your throat.

tell me you love me when i speak my mind
only to scold me for calling out your
half constructed,
weak attempted lies.

you know what?
go ahead and fill up the cup with ice.
i'm not cold for standing here before the world,
while others fiddle with the thimbles
to hang their overly-posed pictures.

forgive me,
for not fitting into
your mood board.
because i am so
goddamn cold.

HOW TO BE AN ARTIST

it's all about holding onto fictitious things
in order to create that inspiring pain.
think back on those dastardly masks they wore,
how they tore you apart all while telling you
that you were whole.

light the match and burn the wax,
seal your skin with the mark
you are convinced
they left behind.

scratch the scabs only to make scars—
this is the beauty of being an artist.

now tear me apart.

SUNSHINE & GROWTH

PLASTIC PLANTS

give me the shears,
these leaves grow too green.
how bountiful and bright,
but they blind my sight.
petals too pretty
ask for a higher price—
for a diligent pair of hands
to pluck the aphids
from my eyes.

if only they knew the truth.
how these colors are made from acrylics,
and these leaves are pasted on with glue.
what you see is only deceit;
i did not earn these blooms.

so give me the blades,
and cut me down to the roots
where i shall start anew.

MISTAKEN DANDELION WEEDS

i made the mistake of allowing hands
to prune the leaves i rooted
from the earliest of my summer days.
green for green,
we exchanged brambles for saw blades.
i watched as they trimmed my tree,
telling me it was too far in the street,
so my neighbors could look
out their balcony window
to watch over their pruned gardens
and overgrown weeds.
the agreements i made grew quieter
with each fallen leaf.

i counted the branches
that used to carry me to the clouds.
fall and sink through the soil
like a stray cat's skeleton;
memories of make believe crack
with each whack of the ax.

they tell me it is because
the wood has gone rotten—
the entire tree will die

if i just sit there and watch it crumble
like the plotline of afterthoughts left to remain
on the notes on my phone.

to remain rooted in rot
is to kill every thought,
so i must remain in my mother's rocking chair
as these men come with their weapons,
tearing my whole garden to shreds
insisting it is infested.

then the rain came one day—
it kept them all away.
cowering and wincing as though it were hail,
the men scattered and shrank
like the accused ants who had been stealing fruit
from my beloved apple tree.

in the wake of the rain and the rubble
of plastic bottles of pesticide,
emerald green sprouts burst through the remnants
of my so-called
disease-ridden leaves.
their veins glimmered with gold,
and in their stems brewed a symphony
of laughter and love.

with their voice,
the sky turned blue and the clouds
flowered like popcorn
in the old family microwave.
seedlings became smiles of blinding light,
asking me to sit down;
pleading for me to stay.

my fingernails filled with soil as i sank beside them,
planting myself in the rain to be
dripping,
drenched.
an unknown thirst had been found and
slowly,
carefully,
quenched.

here i had been allowing strangers
to walk upon my land,
paying them to fix the damages
they had claimed to see;
pulling out dandelion weeds
that were seedlings left behind
from honeybees.
flowers ached to bloom,
but strangers convinced me
they were only annuals—

too weak to shed a petal,
let alone two.

in the craters of my fingers,
i feel the earth and her crust—
everything below and beneath.

it is in the corpse of death,
i have found a home for my roots.
my leaves shall stretch over corners,
tumbling through the windows
of growling neighbors.

their words shall fall on deaf ears because,
who said i asked you?

this is my home.
these hands you see,
they have held life and death,
and will do so again and again.
so who are you to tell me and mother earth
what we should do?

i shall remain rooted in my ideals,
overgrown with boughs
both old and new.

you can sharpen your garden pliers and your axe,
but these branches of mine are infinite;
they are divine.

you cannot stop me from spreading
like the swarm of locusts
you cried were a curse.
i am the breath of wild,
granting myself calm
within the great storm.

MIDNIGHT MOTH

i caught a cocoon left in the soil.
found like the hollowed remains
of orange peels after a soccer game;
remnants of a life that was,
and is,
and will be.

i watched it with curiosity,
looking for a flutter of wings,
a rainbow of colors collected
from the decibels of mother nature
and her delectable symphony.
yet it sat still,
appearing dead to the naked eye.

collected with dirt-stained fingernails—
a childlike delicacy—
i plucked the creature's home from its nest,
placing it in a jar for my own selfish keeping.
i poked the glass each hour of the day,
waiting for it to flower—
to spread its wings.

i wanted to see life;
i wanted to see what it was like.

one day the cocoon cracked.
out came spots and stripes,
speckled with fuzz and tiny black legs.
i knew in its flight this was no souvenir,
like my favorite glass teddy bear.
it was alive;
it deserved a life.

so up goes the raspberry red lid
and out goes the flurry of small wings.
up towards the stars,
to the shimmering white face—
the mother of the night.

gone in the whisk of the wind,
a beauty of the night sacrificing itself
to find the light,
while i lay softly in the darkness,
commanded by the swarm of words in my head
not to move or say another thing,
like the carcass of the empty of cocoon—
a body that never grew wings.

i've sat for years now,
deep in the dark,
silent like the holy night,
going cold as though

i was made of stone.
i wondered,
why must i remain in this darkness?

if a moth is willing to forfeit its life
in the search of even the
smallest speck of light,
i can scorch the earth;
i can be the light.

CURLING AT THE EDGES

we work diligently to grow
leaves of our own—
pretty petals to flaunt for the bees.
but no matter the soil,
our roots only stand in the sunshine.
those colorful dresses and emerald green leaves
wilt and fade,
rusting with age.

not even the prettiest of gardens
can avoid the scythe of time.
yet we push through the dirt,
through the skeletons of those before us,
saying we can grow more leaves,
more petals—
that we can live longer
than the rest.

we must understand
that beauty will never last.
we are a cycle:
a chain of events
that are destined to befall.

grow your leaves without a care,

because you only have them
for so long.

ROOT ROT

my tears have spilled
from the heart of los angeles
to the crest line of bluff cove.
the sunshine has filled me up and shattered
the fragile state of my bones.
like a tree crafted for the brisk winds of winter,
my limbs rot and remain hollow.
withered leaves dance in the backyard
of suburban homes
where new and old friends roam;
swept up on highway five trying
to find a place of rest and content.

i failed to realize my sorrows
were giving birth to the land.
my sobs have soaked the soil
beneath my calloused feet
to grace the morning with tender sprouts
left to be harvested
for the next generation.

the weathering effects of my emotions
were not damaging the home within my heart,
but building a new field to plant new ideas:

greater thoughts of love and life and living.

i shall let myself cry to feed the roots of the earth;
i shall shout my anger to give breadth
to the pollinated winds.

my sorrow is the most meaningful piece
of my existence.

UNDER THE BLUE MOON

in the eyes of the sky,
find a reflection glaring back
from the ever deep.

from black to blue,
connect the stars to create a map
of the places you wish to forget.
in the shapes,
find echoes of the girls and boys
you used to know.
how tiny those eyes make you feel—
a mere speck of dust
in a storm of stardust.

it is all in the gaze of the beholder.
dive into the deep sea,
breath held for almost too long,
but before the universe
goes completely black and blue,
stare deep into the abyss
that has been dangling
so far above you.

years at a time,
all while you ask,

why?

gazing back ever so gently,
despite the treacherous fear,
you shall see them:
so fragile and delicate in this darkness
in which they told you to hide.

find your footing and spread your wings,
for the most beautiful treasure of this world,
is the adoration of your soul;
knowing in growth,
you have survived
the deep black and blue.

now it is only time
for the stars,
all designed from
the most tender threads
of your heart.

NOT SO SMALL SOUTH BAY TOWN

i used to call myself lucky
for garnering the attention of a pretty face.
according to the movies,
only beautiful people fall
for a beautiful face.

they wear each other on their right finger
as a promise not to each other,
but to themselves as a reminder
to maintain their social media screen.
everyone thinks they are in love,
or the entire reality will fall apart.

to look in the mirror alone
presents only smudged shadows
and ribbons of undesired,
stretched out skin.

feel that groping, possessive touch
of your dearly attractive lover?
that means they are captivated by you—
you should be flattered,
not nauseous at the way they invaded your space
when you were on the brink of sleep and awake.

they are the name that circulates
hotel room parties and the face that lingers
in the back of every instagram picture.

they chose to put their hands
and their lips around and against you.
this must make it special—
it must make it real,
because they could have anyone,
but for some reason,
they chose you.

so forget the lies,
or the wandering eyes,
or the lack of attention
to your depressed,
pleading for help kind of texts—
they are beautiful according to the mirror and
everyone else around you.

it took many months,
but i decided to wipe the mirror clean.
in its reflection,
i see a sad, small girl
who was seeking validation
from pretty los angeles boys who relied only
on their bathroom-lighted selfies.

i convinced myself to be special,
not because of my talents or my achievements,
or the loving bonds i've garnered,
but because a societally-attractive boy looked at me
a little longer than others.

this is all quite laughable now.
i don't need to look in the mirror
to see my existence.
the validation i was seeking
could never be fulfilled
by a mannequin trying to find life
within the essence inside of me.

everything i was missing was found
deep within the shell of my skin.
in the ugly, pulsing pink
fleshy parts of muscle and tissue
the world refuses to acknowledge even exists.

temporary approval from a pre-wrinkled,
sun-spotted face,
with words seeping through teeth
that will likely go yellow
with the alcohol and drugs you throw back
as though the concept of aging
doesn't exist.

that face is fleeting, honey;
the hunger of the heart is everlasting.

let's see who withers first.

WINDOW SHOPPING

before you decide to swipe right
on the idea of the girl you've so swiftly carved
into the recesses of your mind,
from gazing at my first picture,
when my hair was longer and my eyes
were a little brighter,
i ask you to find a box of something flammable—
some form of tinder.
instead of sparking a dream
with your smoke shop lighter,
step into your local antique market
where you can find a box of genuine
wooden .

maybe you've forgotten what it feels like
to scrap the sandpaper while muttering prayers
for even the slightest ember,
only to bathe yourself in the warmth
of a divine fire.

you've lost your love for the sparks
and have fallen into the lust
of an oil induced fire.
gone is the desire for the marathon
that pours from the love

of a handmade hearth,
replaced instead by pot-smoke smeared bonfires.

don't mistake me for your latest kindling—
i am the tinder that forms the ufo-like light
you catch glimpses of
in the pitch of night,
when your neighbors are asleep
and you've closed your rickety plastic blinds.
the tinder you confuse me for
being a fantasy of your mind—
you're a whore for a happily ever after,
but refuse to remain through the thrush
of third degree burns.

i am not your bundle of sticks
to blow into a fire,
to light your campsite—
to keep you and your dreams warm
in the dark cold.
it's all smoke and mirrors
when you choose the spark of an ember
without even the slightest scar.

go ahead and fill your mind
with the puppet show of your perfect girlfriend who
saves you from your downfall,

uncaring as she falls apart.

burn bitter with scorn for the fallen lovers
you said were star crossed.
i'll be sitting here with my matches,
staying warm in the icy cold.

THE WRITER'S WAR

i'm sorry to tell you this,
but there's a chance if you meet me,
i'll turn you into my latest
midnight poetry.

even if you knew me in the previous decade,
chances are i remember all those beautiful
and terrible things you said.
like the dried up acrylic paintings
on my vanity mirror,
i've collected all those consonants and vowels
in each bristle and brush stroke
as a constant reminder of the disappointment
i was to you.

throw me like the dandelion you plucked
from your garden,
to make a wish you'd forget
by sunset.
a whisper of words you speak to be heard—
to distract from the fact
we're no longer friends.

i carry the hurt across my back
with the dictionary of lackluster definitions

i've created from the pain of misspoken words
and too-late apologies.
my error was erasing the sentences
of self reflections—
i wrote only of the delays in anger;
painted the suppressed pain in hopes
it would all go away,
while memories of my face are forgotten
by my brothers, sisters, and lovers,
who promised to always
remain by my side.

i scramble for the shards of your perceptions
to build myself back together—
to fit the picture of the sad-eyed girl
you stood beside in your favorite picture of us.

there i go,
writing new words,
trying to tell others what it means
to fear being forgotten with such intensity,
you slit the tips of your fingers
until the paper drips from edge to edge
with the crimson i thought no longer
to have remained.

if you wonder why

everyone says writers are lonely and depressed,
it is because we haven't found the words
of what we're trying to say next.

for too long,
i carried pages of my feelings,
trying desperately to explain it to others
who worried about how often
i cried at night.

my error, i now see,
was trying to tell others
how it felt to feel unexplainable emotions
that could never possibly be explained
with words of the dictionary.

my pain
is inexplicably wonderful and incomplete.
through being forgotten by others,
i remember ways of loving myself
through my own eyes,
not through past friends or lovers.

my emotions are endless
like the lust for new found words
that may never exist.
it is invisible,

and though previously displaced,
i've learned to turn the mirage of broken pieces
into the silhouette of the woman
i am and know i can be.

i write for myself,
collect my tears and use them as ink,
as my love for the world and fellow lost souls
lay beneath as my indestructible
land of parchment.

this is why i've turned you into my poetry,
not to slam you at the next open mic night,
but to live in bliss
with the uneven hems
of my existence.

i am a writer.
every day,
i thank the world for loving me and the people
for trying to lead me astray.

none of you could ever stop me
from falling in love with the pen
and the hand that holds it in place.

AT THE SCISSORS EDGE

i know you don't like my bangs.
it's because i don't look like zoey deschanel
or catherine zeta jones.

sure, yes, of course,
they looked bad when i cut them in high school.
you could see the insecurities
screaming across the rounds of my eyes—
how i kept trying to butcher and change
the blur of lines captured in the wooden frames
my mom liked to have on her bedside.

i dreamed of falling under a knife,
to be split open and rearranged.
i wanted to look like another pretty face
on the trending page—
to garner those little pink hearts;
hundreds of people who lived to adore,
while crying behind their own bedroom door.

but i'm twenty one now.
my body has billowed to break;
my eyes have grown wider
to capture the ugly and the beautiful
of my daily life:

nothing more than a tattering waif
of stained cotton ripped
from seam to seam.

this is how young me would view
the me that is here with you
on these blanched pages.

i look back on those tired eyes of mine
from years ago,
feeling pity for the girl i once was—
someone i thought i knew.
the woman here now
is a patchwork of earth.

i have seen the grotesque of the dirt,
eaten it in spoonfuls to discover
those little pink hearts?
they are worth nothing in a world
with tangible beauty
that can be felt and grasped and held
between calloused fingertips.

to be adored is nothing more
than a cry of a desperate child
to finally be heard.
the soul who scrawls

these scattered portraits
is a girl no more,
but a woman wrapped in quilts.

i would not be here
without these abstract fabrics.
a quilt cannot be made
without the forgotten pieces
humanity decided to leave behind.

i'm happy to be alive,
unbothered by the scraps of myself,
i have torn and burned along the way.

i'm happy to tell you that, yes,
i did cut my own bangs.

A SCREENWRITER'S DAYDREAMS

i am not your manic pixie dream girl.
stop saying i am the girl
of your wildest fantasies and romanticizing
my poor mental health tendencies.
you do not realize
your whipped cream words do nothing
but dehumanize the heart and soul
in which i carry.

these bones rot with trauma and fatigue;
this is perceived as an opportunity
that i will relate to and take away
every morsel of your childhood pain.

my lips have become sewn
because you allowed no room
for my words to take bloom.
my ears ring from the babbling
of your broken hearted past lives.
you only open up a single seam so i can say,
you didn't deserve to be treated that way.

these words are rarely spoken from you.
if they are,
it is only a mere utterance

with the thinness of cardboard,
as to which you seem to think
i am made out of.

i am not the fool i began making myself out to be,
because i begged you
not to idolize me.
my colored hair is not a quirky phase;
my artistic abilities are more than an outlet
of my depression and anxiety.
you refused to listen to reality and instead,
wanted to live in your favorite romantic comedy.
perhaps you were too inebriated to see clearly—
the drunken fools always find their way to me.

i am not medicine for your trauma.
though i have a tendency
to lean towards the most broken,
wanting to heal the wounds i've had
on my very own skin,
it is not my responsibility to raise you.

love is a partnership of two individual humans,
but for too long,
i have been subjected to the objectification
of an archetype,
likely created by another

old, predatory man.

i am not a trophy to hold up
at your sad parties.
i am a human being,
multifaceted with ideas and thoughts
and emotions and likes
and dislikes and hobbies
and—
must i go on?

i am the main character of my own story,
not a plot device to your patriarchal fantasies.

POST-ISOLATION IDEALS

do you think these hands belong to you?
just because they danced along your arms,
held your jaw as i pulled it to mine?
these palms were destined
to dance in the grasp of many,
the tender feathers of my heart
are to be framed above an old poem
i probably dedicated to them.

does this make my love insincere?
i used to think so.

how could this tongue weave whispers
of promises of never ending love to two
within a time of one hand?
i felt wrong for having given away my pieces
to another before you;
guilty for thinking of giving them
to another after i left you.
what was i doing with lips licked pink
to be plucked for the next?

i've questioned who this body belongs to
when all this time,
it was carefully carved for loving me;

for whoever my soul connects to.

no longer shall i carry remorse
of sharing shards on skin
that will eventually regenerate
and forget about you.

i want to love,
even knowing it will end
with one of us tearfully sharing a goodbye.
we will never love another,
not exactly how it was with each other.

i now realize this is okay;
this is the beauty of love and
being alive.

MAIN CHARACTER SYNDROME

instead of writing another poem of anger,
i wish to digest the reality of how i am the evil
to my own plot-line.

the enabler of negative thoughts,
i chew on delusions of being
the topic of conversations;
an object found from the curbside
to observe and criticize.
miscommunications carry
through my nightmares
to mold into daydreams
where friendly conversations
are a sign that,
i think, maybe,
they do like me.

my hands are desperate
as they grapple for fibs and fictitious friction
between myself and this old friend of mine.
as i curl into a carcass in the dead of night,
to convince myself i am small.

my breath fogs the windows of bars
snagged along the coastline,

reeking of validation from others
to reel me away from my own existence.
i'm drunk off of pointless complaints that in truth,
mean nothing to me,
though my detachment from reality
has led me to believe
lies from my friends in middle school
are the reason for my hardened exterior
and deep-rooted trust issues.

i thread riddles of my past into my present
to remind myself of why i am broken;
to explain to others that my lack of selflessness
is an offspring of my teenage tragedies.

i spit fire from my tongue in disgust
of the shallowness of the people
in los angeles county,
but the only forests i burned with these words
were the woods barricading the rotting roots
of my individual existence.

in the wake of the ashes i told myself
i had risen from again and again,
i instead discovered nests of embers
knotted in the soil,
stretching up

to my favorite bundles of leaves.

it took two decades to realize
the gasoline had been set alight
by the hands that held my face while i sobbed,
where did it all go wrong?

it began with me,
with my decision to discuss problems
that do not even exist—
to liven up my tragedies and continue
to carry them with me,
all to avoid the corners i've sharpened
to hurt myself and unknowingly,
others.

this is why i used to take everything personally:
because i lacked the ability to live authentically
in fear of being faced with the thoughts
that loom over me in the quiet moments
of the daytime.

i became the main character of mine
and everyone's else story,
all while convincing myself
i had become a prop in the background
of the world around me.

one could say the side effects of los angeles
had gotten to me, but in an honest,
bones split open,
self-evaluation,
i have simply been too frightened and weak
to consider the upheaval of learned thoughts,
which would normalize my human existence.

by developing a hunger
for wanting to be special,
i became the very person
in which, i would criticize;
in which, i would despise.

i have grown to dislike myself in an honest manner,
but rather than taking this as another opportunity
to dwell on selfish guilt,
i have chosen to follow the road
where my most raw and hollow parts
have been strewn,
in order to put myself
back together.

i am learning to rest in silence
so i may finally hear the main characters
in the entire library of stories.

A LETTER FROM YOUR MEDICATION

dear friend:

i am writing to tell you that i have decided to shut off the depressed daydreams of your mind. i found a mirror next to your thoughts, and at first, it didn't make sense. how could this glass—something so sharp, heavy, and deadly—live among the land of sweet dreams, where love blossoms and new ideas spring?

when i looked in, i only found shadows in the glass, stirring like ants waiting for the next haunting footprint. the darkness stood on edge, shivering while trying to gnash its sharpened teeth.

it was then that i began to understand.

this reflection has found its way to you. it insists for you to be something else—someone who is seen by the insecure eyes others admire, failing to see the lack of light. you must look deeper.

see that crack? those broken shards twisting and turning into letters? they cut too deep, feasting as they watch you bleed.

look again now, beyond the broken. don't you see?

these shattered pieces are the remains of the walls
you worked so hard to build. bricks to cage the
broken, and mortar to freeze and forget the mistakes
yourself and others made. do not be fooled by the
allure of the shimmering beauty of the glass—it's all
an act.

in the attached package, i have left you a hammer.
with this, i ask you to find yourself; i ask you to
break the glass. break it, until there is nothing left
but the sound of your breaths. forget the shimmers.

hear the sound of your false reality falling apart?
you're alive again, and you are destined to remain.

> sincerely,
> your friend you forgot to take last thursday.

COASTLINE HORIZON

looking back down a road that is now overgrown
with thickets of willows and withering rose bushes,
the golden hour glow points ahead
to a gleaming stem of light—
a flower made
from the golden drops of the sunshine,
watered by the opalescent tears of the moon.
a garden lies before me,
blooming in colors beyond imagination.

the complexities of the past
stick to my side like thorns,
but if there is one thing i know for certain,
is that i was destined to create.
my heart has never felt fuller
knowing i have a home
in the pages of my journal and
the scattered array of sticky notes
in my broken drawer.

my characters have granted me courage
when i thought myself to be weak.
they have shown me a rare source of wisdom
when i failed to see eye to eye with another,
refusing to see the problem

remained within myself,
not the other.

i have to tell you,
i didn't think i'd be alive at this time—
even high school seemed like a dream
from someone else's mind—
though in the encasement of leather bound spines,
i've found a purpose:
a platform to live and die.
my keyboard gives me sustenance,
like the sun and moon
give life to the flowers before me.

while i still wander this road,
unsure of who i should allow to follow
or where exactly i am meant to go,
i'm lucky to have a garden in my eyes.
a passion so incredibly,
breathtakingly beautiful,
i lose myself in its glory.

i cry in its divinity,
knowing i could never
leave this life.

how could i?

i could never
leave my characters,
not without their stories
being told.

NICE TO MEET YOU

forgive me for who i have been.
many things i've said up until now
have been spoken out of what felt like
societal obligation.

i spoke on behalf a broken-hearted child
who chose to never release unspoken pains
that have grotesquely aged.
no longer can i recognize what was said
in the first place,
that dislodged my faith
in the human race.

the leading performance of my adolescent play
was stunt doubles to catch the falls
that were meant to forsake me.
regardless of my stance being balconies
away from the stage,
i felt and collected every droplet of pain
to add to my keepsake jar of reasons why
i cannot trust anybody.

this has been a tragic disservice
to those who have stumbled through
the doorway of my presence;

it is even a greater injustice
to my own individual existence.

what a dull life it is sitting against
the cold wall of bricks
that have been stacked so high,
i cannot recall the last time i saw the sky.
so afraid of the billboard proclamations
of mistakes and misplaced faith,
i swiftly forget about the humans
who printed and painted the signs
in the first place.

i lived with such shame of being a human,
i have forgotten others existed between me;
my love has been retained with hazard,
contained in solitude to be perused solely by
my own tired eyes.

i've grown exhausted of living in this shell
of what i thought to be a cocoon,
but was a facade for my own fears
to excuse myself from living a life,
in hopes of escaping any form of pain.

i am choosing now
to remove myself from my ego—

to talk to strangers without desire,
to give gifts without reason,
to write notes without cause.

there are lives outside of mine.
i think it is time for us all
to finally
be intertwined.

THE END IS OVER

the past is a shadow.
i cut it from my tree and now,
i am free.

ACKNOWLEDGMENTS

The Los Angeles Gardening Guide would have likely sat on the digital shelves among my other manuscripts for another six years without the endless love and support of my family: my mom, dad, brother, and of course, my sister, Bobbi Haas, who showed me the beauty of the written word. Not many people would support their daughter or sibling spending countless days and nights writing without seeing any source of income or a future to build on, but my family sat beside me through it all—mental breakdowns, happy tears, and strange ideas about the world and our existence.

Thank you to the friends I've made along the way, who inspired me with their own art and passions. Thank you to my poetry professor, Dana Crotwell, for guiding me through difficult times with the beauty of language, and giving me the confidence to pursue writing when I had just begun to give up. Thank you to the Redondo Poets Society for hosting an open platform for artists to have their voices heard—I don't know if I would have continued to write poetry if it wasn't for the support of Jim and the same faces that showed up every Tuesday night. Thank you to the El Camino College Zine Club for inspiring to follow my passions in school and connecting me to artists who continually inspire me to be a better writer and person. Thank you to Deidre Book for opening your home to me to allow a space to meticulously create and demolish and recreate this book, and teaching me how valuable it is to be independent and curious.

Thank you to everyone I've encountered along the way. The majority of this work was written when I was twenty-years-old, and a few from twenty-one. It is both painful and liberating to release a series of work that encapsulates a pivotal age in my life, in which I can now look back on and remind myself the importance of my growth—to embrace the light and dark of life.

The Los Angeles Gardening Guide will stand as a reminder to remain thoughtful, kind, and open-minded as I further peruse my twenties.

MEET THE AUTHOR

Thea Rosemary is a twenty-two year old writer originally from the South Bay of California, and is now dwelling in the city of Los Angeles, California. Writing for the last six years, Thea found peace and passion for the craft, creating novel-length works of various forms of fiction. She then began creating poetry and zines (mini magazines) over the last two years, publishing two independent works—*best of tears* and *clippits*—featuring her original poetry, digital art, and photography.

Thea has been published in the El Camino Creative Arts Journal, *The Myriad*, twice. (The first feature work is formerly published under her legal name, Taylor Barbour). She was also selected as a featured poet for the Redondo Poets Society, presenting a twenty-minute reading of her own original poetry. Thea managed to sell around 100 physical copies of the first independent printing of *The Los Angeles Gardening Guide*, landing in a few select stores within Los Angeles and the South Bay.

Thea dreams of writing many works of fiction and non-fiction, hoping to bring a healing, expansive perspective of living, and a raw medium of inspiration to help bring unity to humankind and the earth.

Social: @thea.rosemary
Email: thearosemary@gmail.com

Photo by: Kevin Kim - @qevinqim

www.ingramcontent.com/pod-product-compliance
Lightning Source LLC
Chambersburg PA
CBHW062052290426
44109CB00027B/2804